HAPPY ? BIRTHDAY

by TONI GOFFE

First published in Great Britain by
Pendulum Gallery Press
56 Ackender Road, Alton, Hants GU34 1JS

HAPPY BIRTHDAY
ISBN 0-948912-12-X

REPRINTED 1991

PRINTED IN GREAT BRITAIN BY
UNWIN BROTHERS LTD, OLD WOKING, SURREY

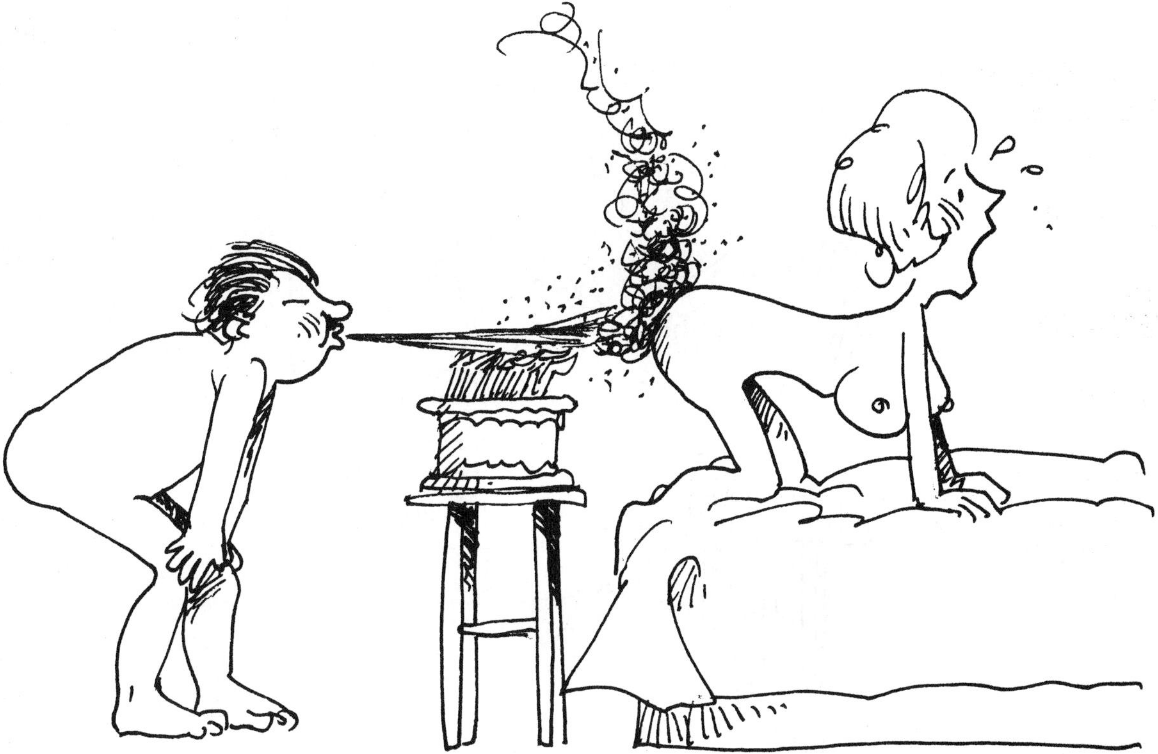

'HAPPY BIRTHDAY TO YOOOOOOOH!'

HAPPY · HIC · BIRTHDAY · HIC · TO ME · HIC!!
HAPPY · HIC · BIRTHDAY · HIC TO ME HIC!!

'NO DEAR, JUST BLOW OUT THE CANDLES...'

'WOULD YOU LIKE TO TRY A CIGARETTE ?..'

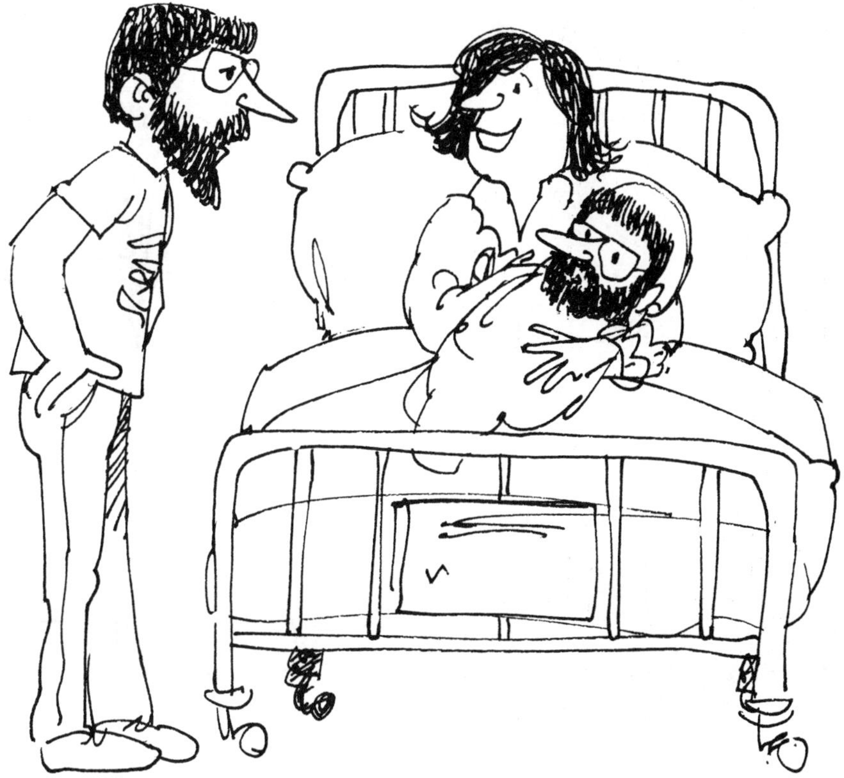

'LOOK, HE'S GOT YOUR NOSE'

'IT'S A SURPRISE FOR YOUR BIRTHDAY, DAD!'

HOW DO YOU KNOW IT'S MY BIRTHDAY?
WERE YOU THERE?

' JOHN, THIS IS YOUR FATHER ... '

'WELL, IT IS HIS BIRTHDAY, GEORGE, AND THAT'S WHAT HE WANTED.....'

'HAPPY BIRTHDAY, PASS IT ON....'

WHAT WAS THE SURPRISE YOU GOT FOR MY BIRTHDAY?
GET THE TEA AND I'LL TELL YOU!..

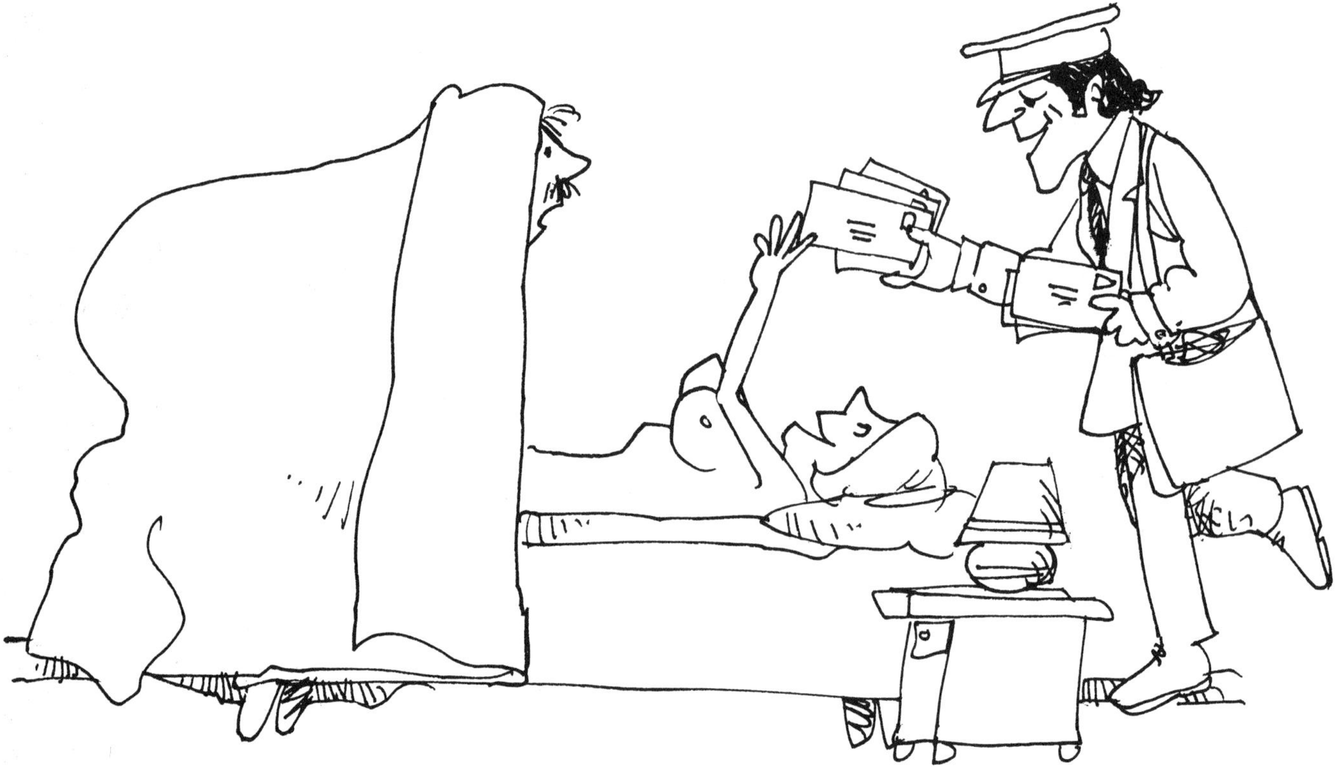

'MORNING ANGELA, JUST BROUGHT UP YOUR BIRTHDAY CARDS ....'

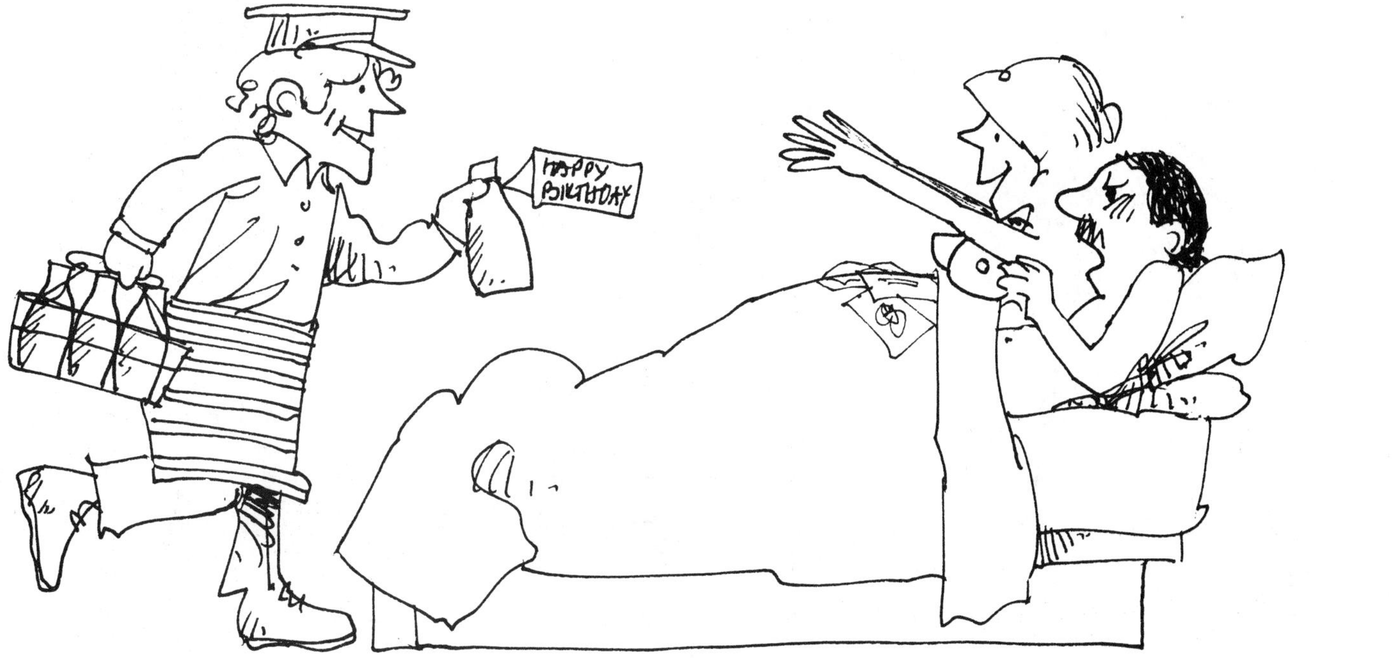

'OH EXCUSE ME SIR, I JUST POPPED UP TO GIVE YOUR WIFE HER FREE PINT FOR HER BIRTHDAY!'

HAPPY BIRTHDAY FIDO X!

'OH, IT'S ALRIGHT, IT'S HER BIRTHDAY!'

'MORE CHOCOLATES!! WHAT ARE YOU TRYING TO DO, FATTEN ME UP FOR CHRISTMAS...'

'IT'S ALRIGHT DAD, IT'S JUST YOUR BIRTHDAY PRESENT, I DIDN'T WANT IT TO GET WET!'

'YES, THAT'S RIGHT... 33 CANDLES....
– WILL YOU QUIT THAT LAUGHING?!!...'

'OH, IT'S **JUST** THE FLOWERS IS IT?'

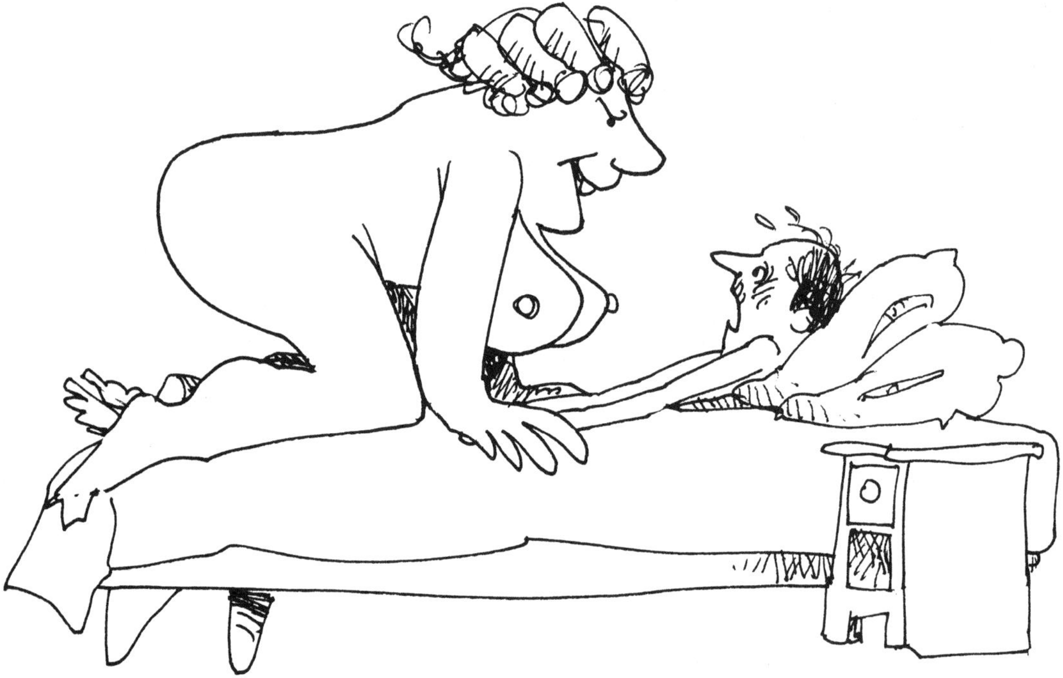

'DO YOU WANT TO CELEBRATE YOUR BIRTHDAY ONE MORE TIME ...?.'

' HI GEORGE! THE WIFE STILL AWAY ?
—— I'VE COME TO HELP YOU CELEBRATE!!..!.

'YOU MIGHT HAVE HID MY PRESENT DOWN HERE SOMEWHERE......'

'AH! I'VE JUST THOUGHT OF A GOOD WAY TO MAKE YOU TELL ME WHERE MY PRESENT IS...'

'OH, IT'S JUST A BIRTHDAY PRESENT I GOT MYSELF IN CASE YOU FORGET.....'

'TAKE NO NOTICE, HE ALWAYS GOES A LITTLE MAD ON HIS BIRTHDAY...'

'HAPPY BIRTHDAY, DEAR, THAT SHOULD SLOW YOU DOWN A BIT...'

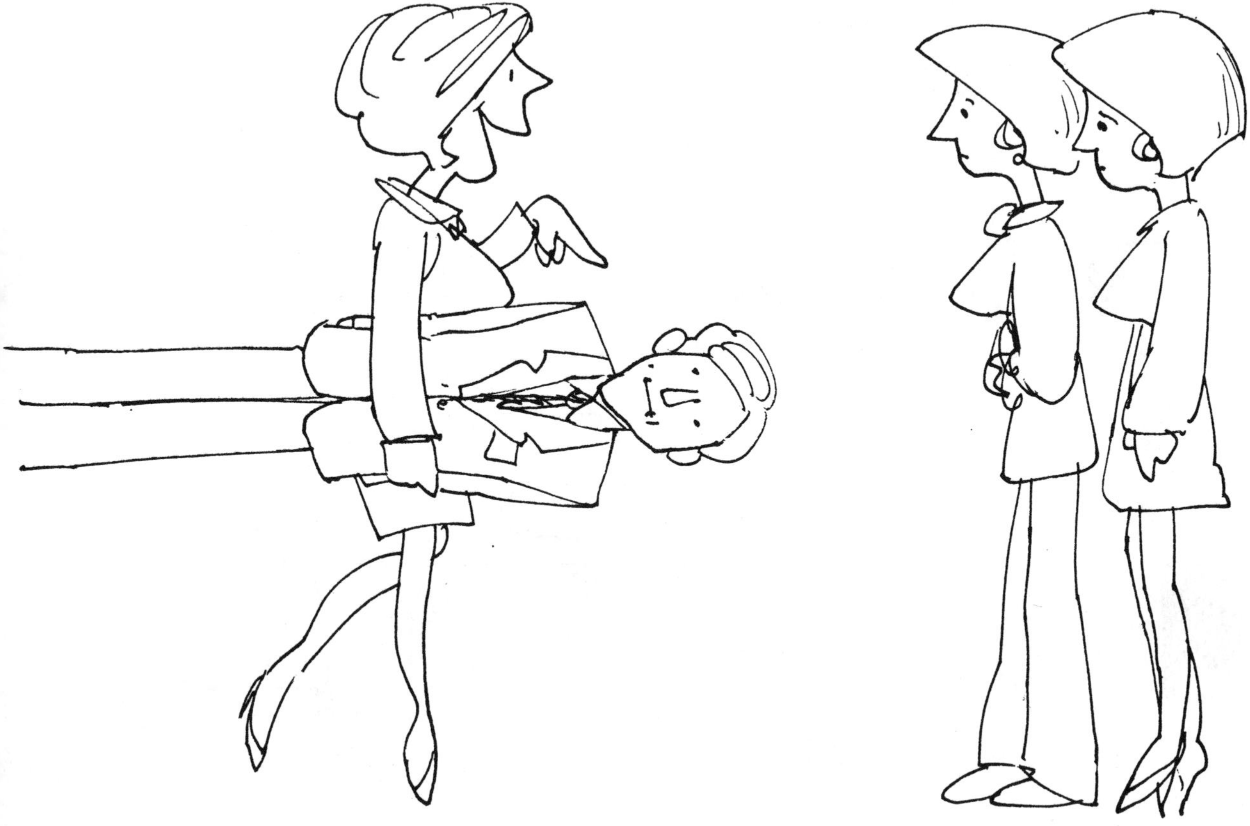

'LOOK WHAT I GOT FOR MY BIRTHDAY...'

'OH DEAR, I THINK IT MIGHT BE MR BARNE'S BIRTHDAY TODAY ....'

'THE BOSS SAID HE WAS GOING TO GIVE ME A BIG SURPRISE ON MY BIRTHDAY...'

'OH NO, WAIT! IT'S NOT TILL NEXT MONTH!'

'BIRTHDAY BUMPS, IS AN OLD TRADITION IN THIS COMPANY MISS JONES'

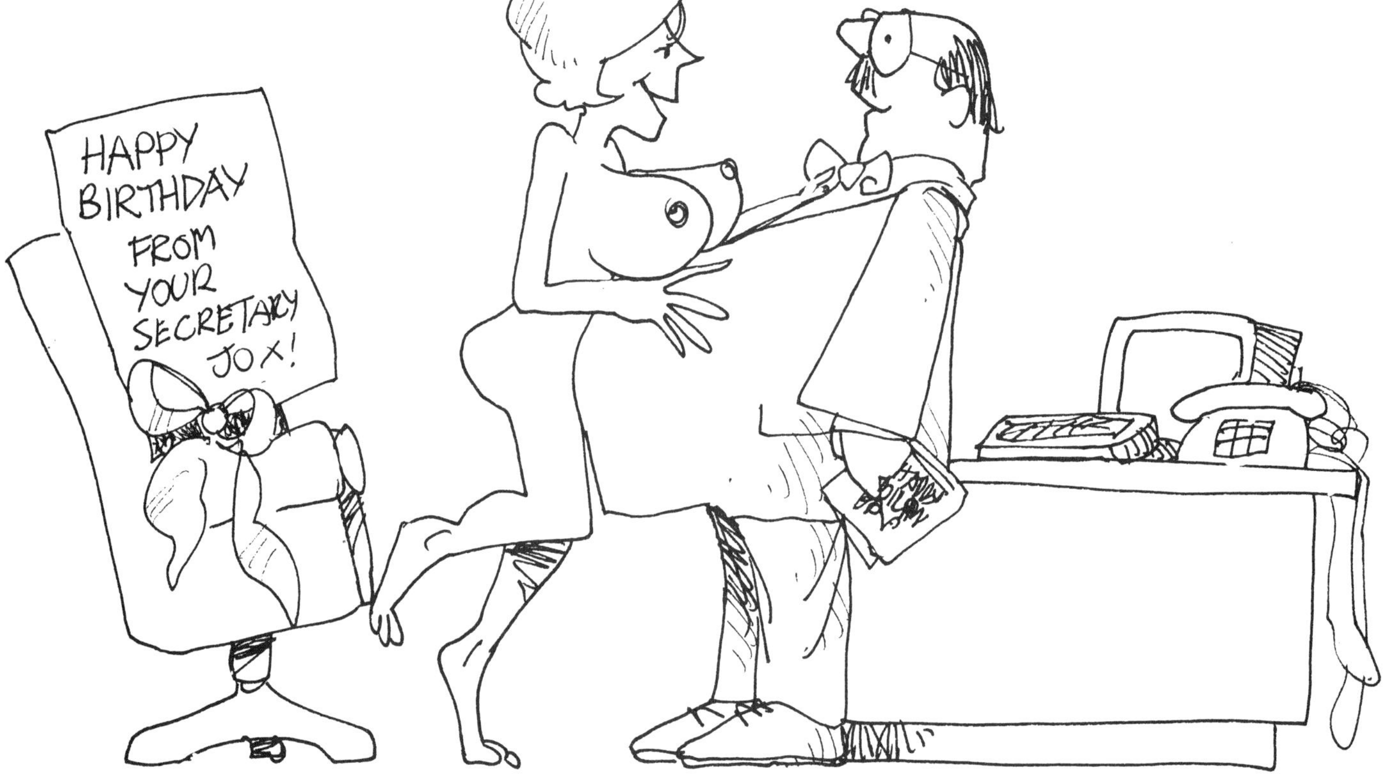

'HOW WELL WE FIT TOGETHER MR SMYTH....'

'WELL, Mr SMITH HOW WOULD YOU LIKE TO CELEBRATE YOUR BIRTHDAY WITH ME....'

'WELL, AT LEAST, YOU'VE GOT THE SUIT RIGHT!!'

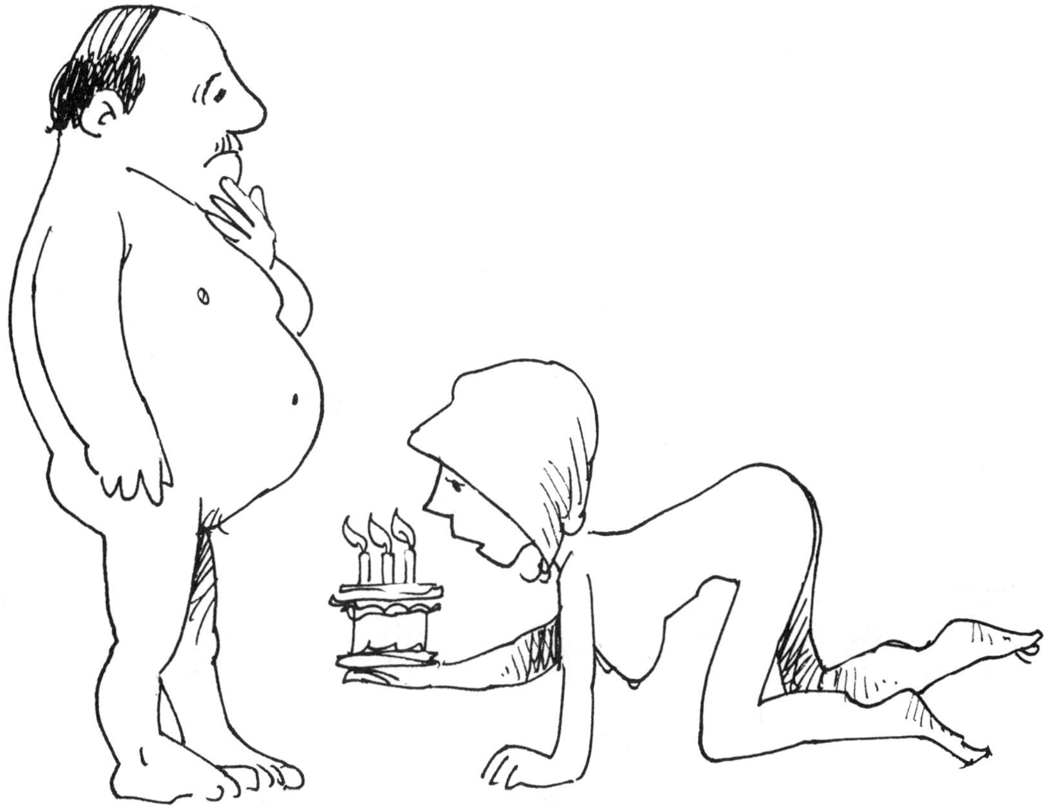

'I'LL SEE IF I CAN SEE IT WITH THE LIGHT FROM THESE CANDLES ...'

'THAT'S NOT QUITE WHAT I MEANT BY A BLOW-JOB MISS JONES....

'HAPPY BIRTHDAY, SIR HENRY, WE'RE FROM BLACKMAIL-O-GRAM......'

'WELL, ARE WE HAVING A CANDLE ON THIS BIRTHDAY OR NOT?'

'OH DEAR, I FORGOT TO GET YOU A CARD!'

YOUR BIRTHDAY CAKE IS IN MY LOVER!
SEE YOU IN COURT
BYE MARTHA X!

HAPPY BIRTHDAY TO ME! LOOKS LIKE I'M THE LAST ONE STANDING, BOYS.....

" AS IT'S YOUR BIRTHDAY YOU CAN COME OUT AND PLAY...."

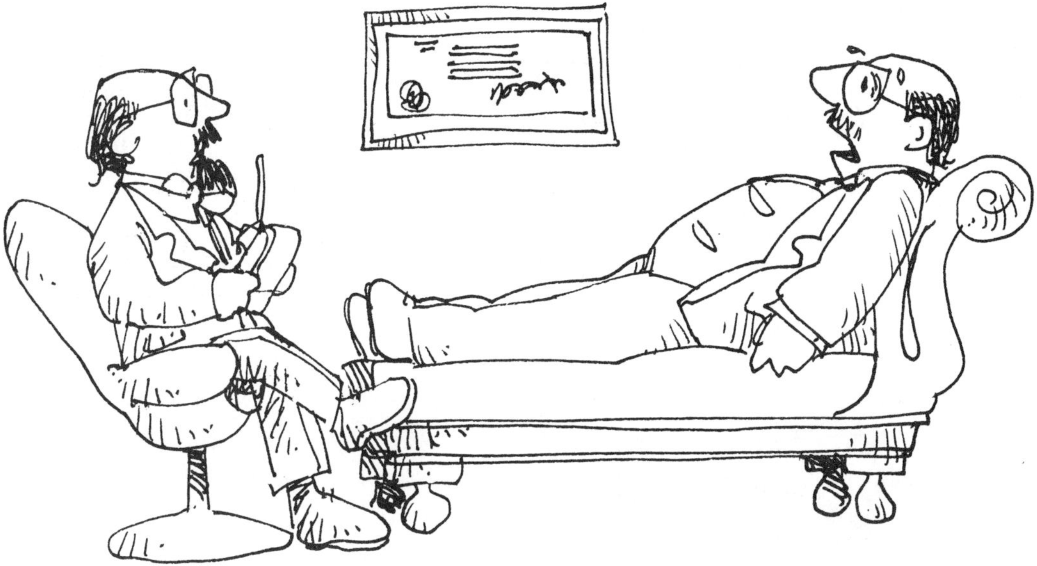

' MY BIRTHDAYS ARE SPEEDING UP!!.!..

'MY BIRTHDAY? NO! WE'RE CELEBRATING MY WIFE'S BIRTHDAY!'

'HE'S A DULL-BUSINESSMAN-O-GRAM, —
— MY HUSBAND SENT HIM...'

'YES, WE ARE SEPARATED, BUT WE ALWAYS CELEBRATE MY BIRTHDAY TOGETHER...'

'SURPRISE, SURPRISE, YOU DIDN'T KNOW I KNEW IT WAS YOUR BIRTHDAY.....DID YOU?'

'WAKE UP DEAR, IT'S TIME TO START THE CELEBRATIONS FOR YOUR BIRTHDAY.....'

'SURPRISE! I'VE BROUGHT SOME MEMBERS OF MY NUDE-LADIES-GROUP-SEX-CLUB TO HELP CELEBRATE YOUR BIRTHDAY..'

'29th FEBRUARY!! WELL THAT MAKES YOU ONLY 25! GOOD, I LIKE YOUNG MEN...'

'I KNOW IT'S FEBRUARY 29th AGAIN ARTHUR, BUT I JUST DON'T FEEL LIKE IT! OK?'

'OH, BAPPY, HIRTHDAY MISS....'

'WE'RE HAVING A LITTLE BIT OF TROUBLE IN THE UPRIGHT-BIRTHDAY-CANDLE-DEPARTMENT......'

'WHEN YOU DO THIS AGAIN SIR, COULD YOU USE FEWER CANDLES?'

'OH, HOW SWEET, HE'S BROUGHT YOU A CARD....'

HAPPY BIRTHDAY TO ME....
HAPPY BIRTHDAY TO ME.....

THANK YOU, JEREMY, FOR FINDING THE TIME TO COME OVER THIS EVENING, AND HELP ME CELEBRATE MY BIRTHDAY....

WHO'S BIRTHDAY ARE WE CELEBRATING TONIGHT, YOURS OR MINE?

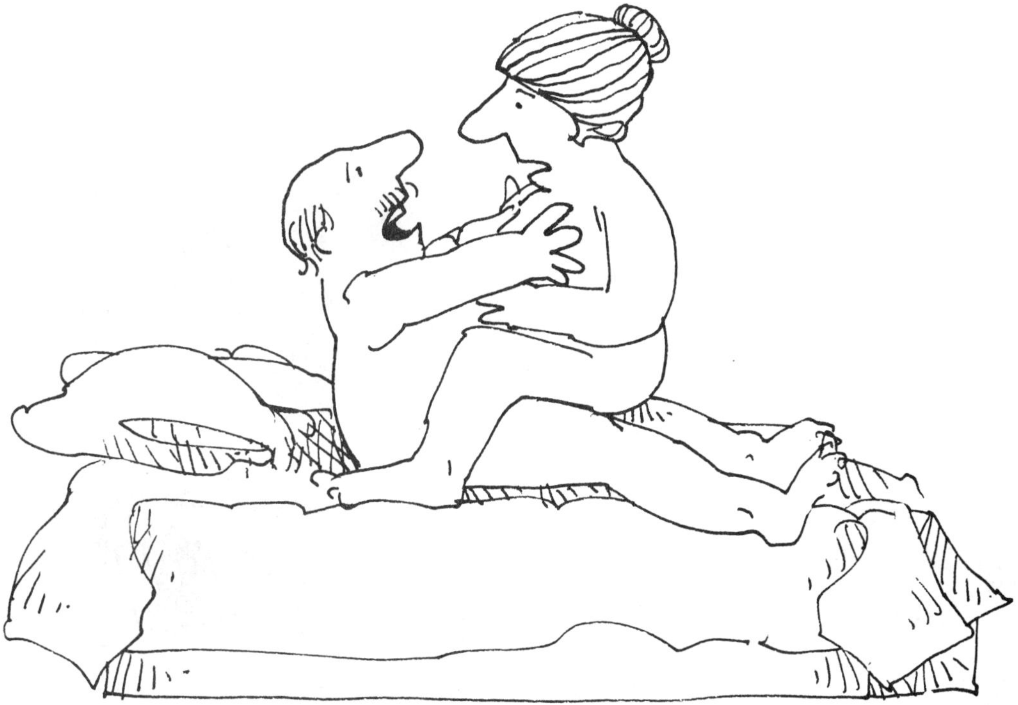

'IT'S BEEN A WHOLE YEAR, I HOPE I CAN REMEMBER HOW TO DO THIS.....'

'SHALL I LIGHT THIS CANDLE NOW?....'

'HAPPY BIRTHDAY, IF YOU'RE STILL THERE....!'

'HAPPY BIRTHDAY TO ME,
HAPPY BIRTHDAY TO ME.......'